Ingatestone and District

in old picture postcards

by
Kenneth Langford

European Library - Zaltbommel/Netherlands MCMLXXXV

GB   ISBN 90 288 3017 0 / CIP

European Library in Zaltbommel/Netherlands publishes among other things the following series:

IN OLD PICTURE POSTCARDS *is a series of books which sets out to show what a particular place looked like and what life was like in Victorian and Edwardian times. A book about virtually every town in the United Kingdom is to be published in this series. By the end of this year about 175 different volumes will have appeared. 1,250 books have already been published devoted to the Netherlands with the title* **In oude ansichten.** *In Germany, Austria and Switzerland 500, 60 and 15 books have been published as* **In alten Ansichten;** *in France by the name* **En cartes postales anciennes** *and in Belgium as* **En cartes postales anciennes** *and/or* **In oude prentkaarten** *150 respectively 400 volumes have been published.*

For further particulars about published or forthcoming books, apply to your bookseller or direct to the publisher.

This edition has been printed and bound by Grafisch Bedrijf De Steigerpoort in Zaltbommel/Netherlands.

INTRODUCTION

Most of the postcards in this book date from the period 1900-1920, and although many of the scenes portrayed are in substance unchanged, they do convey the sense of a way of life long since gone; and perhaps most notably, an absence of traffic.

The villages covered are, in order, Ingatestone, Fryerning, Buttsbury, Margaretting and Mountnessing; of these, the first named is the largest, and lies at the centre of the cluster.

The name Ingatestone is generally thought to have originated from a combination of the words 'Ing' (holding of land) and 'at the stone' (the latter referring to the four pre-ice-age boulders in the area, of which two now stand on the corners of Fryerning Lane and one outside the south door of the church).

The ancient Roman road from London to Colchester runs through the High Street, and because its distance from the capital, 23 miles, was a convenient day's journey by stage coach, the settlement developed as a stopping and changing place for such traffic. Accordingly, the village has always, until fairly recently, had a large number of inns. Their reputation for hospitality was high, and among those who stayed was the diarist, John Evelyn (in 1656 and 1659).

The place prospered, becoming a small town, not only because of an important weekly market and large cattle fair, but also because it was the centre of a flourishing agricultural area. By the 1840's however, and the coming of the railway, it was reduced to the status of a village. Fifty years after this, a traveller wrote of Ingatestone: 'It seems to have fallen asleep when the last coach took its last change and never to have had the energy to waken again!'

The extension of the London commuter area and the pleasant atmosphere and surroundings, plus easy accessibility by rail from Liverpool Street, created in the 1950's and 60's a demand for new houses which brought about the demolition of many larger houses, and the building of new roads and estates. During this time, the Rectory was replaced by Fairfield estate, Nithsdale by Ashleigh Court and The Paddocks, Docklands by Docklands Avenue and adjoining roads, The Chase by Whadden Chase and surrounding roads, and Tor Bryan by the Tor Bryan estate. Open ground or disused sites such as the brickworks, which developed into the Furlongs, were quickly engulfed.

The huge increase in road traffic made congestion such a problem that a northern by-pass was created in 1960 which instantly restored comparative peace to the High Street. The by-pass had another beneficial effect — that of establishing a fixed northern boundary, effectively limiting any expansion of the village in three directions — the railway line forming a southern boundary.

Thus a village 'envelope' exists, permitting new development only as 'infilling' — the whole area outside the 'envelope' being part of the Metropolitan Green Belt.

Two conservation areas have been created, one approximately the full length of the High Street, and the other the Station Lane area including the railway station.

The population of Ingatestone and Fryerning increased only gradually during the nineteenth century (by 35% to 1,748) whereas Greater London in the same period had increased six-fold. The most rapid increase has occurred in the last thirty years, during which time the population has doubled to 4,805.

Chiefly because there was no rapid increase of population, there was no drastic re-building of the High Street such as occurred in many Essex villages, and it was not until the 1960's that any major changes took place. These were only four in number, but regrettably did nothing to add to the character of the village. They were − the building close to the Market Place, of shops and offices and an overbearing mosaic; in place of The Limes, a Bank, shops and flats; in place of the Spread Eagle, shops; and in place of cottages, a large supermarket (Budgens). The mosaic depicts symbolically various episodes in the history of the village, including the visit of Queen Elizabeth I to the Hall, which is the only major event which has ever occurred in Ingatestone or any of its surrounding villages.

Fryerning and Ingatestone have for some as yet unknown reason, always been arbitrarily interlinked. Indeed, until they became one civil parish in 1889 over three quarters of the High Street was legally part of Fryerning Parish. In 1958 the boundaries of the ecclesiastical parishes were rationally redrawn. Fryerning was granted to one of the followers of William the Conqueror, Robert de Gernon. His grandson gave half of the manor and the church to the military order of the Knights Hospitallers who retained it for nearly 400 years until their Order was suppressed. Sir William Berners, a royal auditor, became owner and his descendants sold Fryerning to Sir Nicholas Wadham. Sir Nicholas married a daughter of Sir William Petre, and the couple founded Wadham College in Oxford. The College is still patron of the living and owns much land. The name Fryerning probably originated from the combination of the adjectival form of the word Friar (in reference to the Knights Hospitallers) and 'Ing'.

Margaretting derives its name from the church of St. Margaret, and Mountnessing was originally 'Mountney's Ing'.

Buttsbury is obviously of Saxon origin, the first element almost certainly being a proper name, no doubt of the first major landholder.

Acknowledgements

Grateful thanks to the following who have kindly loaned cards from their collections: B.R. Back, Miss G. Baker, Mrs. Burgess, P. Coverdale, C.H. Cox, J. Cross, Essex Record Office, T.B. Green, D. Healey, P. Hyde, H. King, L. Morgan, A. Radley, Mrs. E. Ransom, P. Smith, L. Sorrell and S. Walde. But particularly to Bob Coe and Dr. Skeoch for their initial loans from their extensive collections, and to the former and his father, W.G. Coe, for their technical help and enthusiasm. Without this co-operation the book would not have been possible.

1. The High Street c. 1830. The earliest pictorial representation. That there was a large number of inns can be seen from the overhanging signs. The almost complete absence of traffic allows the child and the chickens and dogs to wander peacefully. The ladder is leaning against the now-vanished Ship Inn. The coach and horses appear to be stopping at The Spread Eagle. Among the buildings still standing, Berkeley House is distinguished by its protruding columns.

INGATESTONE, HIGH STREET & SMITHY

2. High Street, looking east. In the left foreground is the Smithy which, in 1929, was converted into a sweetshop and was known as the 'Half-Way Shop'. On the extreme right are the former workshouses.

3. High Street, looking east in 1884. A peaceful scene at 8.20 in the morning. A boy is delivering by hand-cart and there is one horse and cart. The houses on the left are still standing, though slightly altered. G.P. Smith's sign and clock are in the distance. Further right are the baker's, Patrick Green's and The Bell. The cottages have since been demolished.

4. The Market Place, looking north. In the centre, with the Esso sign, was Jimmy Westle's garage. The concrete base marks the spot where the village pump stood. The site of the two cottages and telephone booth is now the car park, and on the extreme right foreground, in the High Street, stood The White Hart, now a block of shops and offices with a large mosaic.

5. The Market Place, looking towards the High Street. The White Hart was still standing on the left. Note that there are no buildings on the south side of the High Street.

6. The very centre of the High Street, with The White Hart, one of the major inns of the village, on the left. It had a picturesque interior, with a secret hiding-place. On the right, The Limes. A house had been here for 500 years, changing hands and form many times. It was an inn, a school for young ladies, and successive doctors' surgeries. By 1964 the walls had been made unsafe through continuous traffic, it had woodworm and dry rot, and so was demolished. The Midland Bank, Martins, Green's, and a block of flats were built on the site.

7. The centre of the High Street, but this time taken from the opposite direction to No. 6 and showing the frontage of The White Hart. It also shows a boot repair shop, The Star, E. Camp, boot and shoemaker, and F.W. Anger, China and glass dealer. This latter shop, now selling antiques, was once a butcher's — the rails for hanging the meat are still suspended from the ceiling.

8. High Street in 1894. Again an absence of traffic — just one horse. From left to right: the porch of a private house (now Spectrum), Ingatestone Bazaar, selling toys, with the Jubilee clock above. The cottages in front of the church which have gone, then the bow-fronted shop selling clothes. On the extreme right, The Star and the corner of what is now called Star Lane.

9. High Street in 1894. The stones at the corner of Fryerning Lane can be seen. A group of three shops with steps, the fronts much altered. Further on is The Royal Oak (now Budgen's supermarket). Returning the other side of the road, the sign of The Spread Eagle can be seen, finally The Anchor, since rebuilt, at the corner of Stock Lane.

10. High Street. Previous cards (Nos. 2, 3, 6, 8, 9) had been taken looking towards Margaretting. This one was taken from the opposite direction, 75 years later, and should be compared with the old print (No. 1). The inscription at the top of the card is an error. The view is in fact from the north. The houses on the left were still standing, but they have since been demolished, and the Community Club and car park are on the site.

35933. INGATESTONE: OLD HOUSES.

11. High Street, east end. Mr. Sitch is delivering the post. The three cottages with wooden steps were successfully restored a few years ago.

INGATESTONE TOP END OF TOWN.

12. High Street, the furthest end, looking towards Margaretting. The lodge of Docklands is on the right. The two cottages on the left are now one house.

13. Almshouses. Founded in 1557 in Stock Lane (where two of the houses still stand). The coming of the railway in 1843 meant their re-siting in the High Street. They were rebuilt, in neo-Tudor style, at a cost of £1,400. The photograph shows Canon Roderick Grant (parish priest for thirty years) at what was probably the Armistice celebration of 1919.

INGATESTONE HOUSE SCHOOL

14. Ingatestone House. At the beginning of the century this was a private school for both boarders and day pupils. For some time the building on the right was c. 1964 the Yorkshire Tea Rooms.

15. Infants' School. Built in 1873 in memory of Mrs. Quick who died in 1871. It originally held forty children, but was extended. It was subsequently demolished, and a new school was built in The Furlongs. On the vacant site a library was opened in 1974. The round stone 'In Memoriam 1871' above the window is preserved on the wall of the new school. A similar stone of the Boys' School (see No. 36) is also on the wall. The boundary brick pillars marking the width of the old school are still standing.

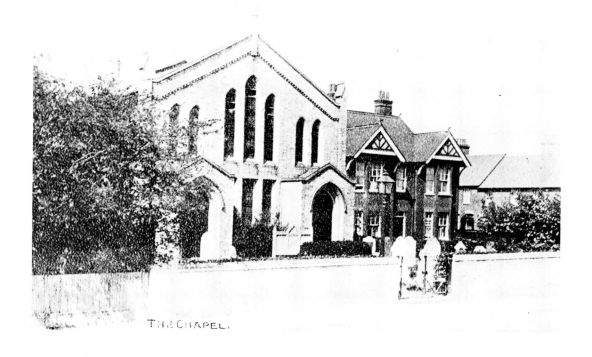

THE CHAPEL.

16. Congregational Chapel. The first chapel was erected in 1812. The present chapel, with a well-proportioned front in white brick, with seven lancet windows, replaced the original 28 years later. It cost £700. It is similar in style to that of Billericay, and was designed by the same architect. In 1972, with the national merger of Congregationalists and Presbyterians, the chapel became part of the United Reformed Church.

17. Celebrating the coronation of Edward VII in 1902. This was a big event, with gifts of beef and groceries to 'cottagers'. There were fireworks, a bonfire, and a torchlight procession. The Crown has a continuous history as an inn, probably over 500 years. Note the letters 'E' and 'R' illuminated by electric light bulbs. The Shuttleworths in addition to running the inn also announced 'Horses and carriages of every description on hire. Conveyances meet all trains'.

18. Spread Eagle — Commercial Inn and Posting House. An important inn where coaches changed horse, and where mail was delivered and collected twice a day. Most of the cricket lunches and social functions were held here. Between the two houses was the entrance to a large cobbled yard; closed in 1963 before demolition — to be replaced by a nondescript block of shops and offices. Pevsner, writing in 1956, said the early Victorian lettering should specially be noticed.

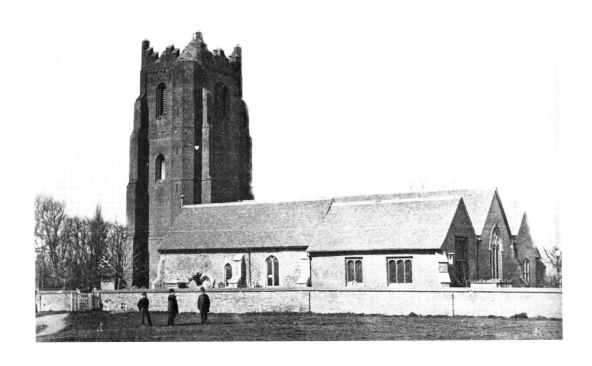

19. Ingatestone Church. Photograph taken from Fairfield. A scene unaltered for almost a century, except for the low brick wall, which has disappeared. The Tudor bricks and windows of the south chapel contrast with the earlier flint and pebble rubble of the south aisle. The tower is considered one of the finest in Essex. Note the two top-hatted, frock-coated policemen.

20. Ingatestone Church. Interior, around 1905 — the curtains were drawn across the windows for warmth. After the magnificent tower, the inside of the church comes as something of a disappointment, since it is without any distinctive features. It is only when one approaches the chancel that the impressive monuments to the Petre family and others are seen.

21. Old Post Office around 1900 with Mrs. Stuart, postmistress, and staff. It had been the home of William Whichcord, the musical postmaster — 'which responsible office he held for 38 years with zeal and ability'. The date of the building, 1720, is carved on a brick on the side wall. It became a cycle shop owned by Mrs. Goodwin and then Wells and Kings. The new post office was built in 1916.

22. The Working Men's Club and Reading Room was started in 1862 by the Reverend L. Parkin, Rector of Ingatestone. The members met in various premises until in 1888, when, with increased membership, a special building was erected to the designs of George Sherrin (see No. 43). The cost amounting to £860, was met by subscription. It was described as an 'ornament to the town'. In addition to a hall there was a library and a reading room. This photograph shows the side of the club before the present hall was built.

23. Aerial photograph of the centre of the village in the early 1960's. The High Street runs from The Spread Eagle to Warders, the bakers. The old rectory and its extensive grounds are seen behind the church. The field opposite the rectory is now occupied by Ingleton House. The Limes and its gardens were still standing, but The White Hart opposite had gone.

NEW BY-PASS, INGATESTONE

24. Aerial view taken c. 1960 during the building of the by-pass. The foreground shows the new A 12, and on the left the cross-over at Fryerning Lane. The Meads is in the right background and Trimble Close and Disney Close are on the left.

NORTON ROAD, INGATESTONE.

25. Norton Road was the first and only road of artisans' houses. Built in 1901/02 by Tom Green on land owned by Edgar Norton Disney of the Hyde. Norton was a family name, the Disneys having come from Disney Norton in Lincolnshire.

26. Station Lane. An almost completely rural scene, looking towards the High Street. In the distance on the right can be seen the end of Avenue Terrace, and on the far right the backs of the Almshouses.

27. Fryerning Lane. The first Council houses to be built in Ingatestone. Taken c. 1920, with a model 'T' Ford van on the left.

The Chase Inter...

28. The Chase. Built c. 1910 as a private house, it later became a hotel, very well known to travellers on the old A 12 before the advent of the by-pass. It had a restaurant, a large banqueting hall, and a very popular swimming-pool open to the public. Demolished to make way for Whadden Chase and adjoining roads.

29. Tor Bryan c. 1886 and now the Tor Bryan estate. Sebastian Henry Petre lived in Tor Bryan House, named after the Devon village (from which William Petre, the family's founder, came). He gave a plot of land adjacent to his property in the Roman Road for the building of the Roman Catholic Church in 1936.

30. The Gate House in its days of glory. Designed by George Sherrin (see No. 43) for his own occupation in 1884. It had ten bedrooms and a galleried hall. The part of the house facing Station Lane is actually the rear — the photograph shows the front, which looked towards the lake. It was used for a time as a school, has in recent years been severely vandalised, but its future is now assured. It is being converted into flats.

31. Nithsdale. A fairly modern house with a southern boundary wall separating its grounds from the station yard. Its last owner before the development of Ashleigh Court and The Paddocks was Sir Maurice Batho Bt.

32. Ingatestone Hall. The unrestored appearance of the Hall c. 1905 is almost unrecognisable from that of today. The straggling ivy was stripped and brickwork restored by Lady Rasch, mother of the present Lord Petre. He lives in the wing to the right. The north wing (to the left) and the long gallery (centre) are now leased to a firm of architects.

33. Ingatestone Hall Chapel. Originally a small chapel for the household, it was greatly enlarged in the 1860's for the parishioners and had a resident priest. It was demolished, and much of the furnishings (including the stained-glass windows made in 1907 by the famous firm of Morris and Company) were used in the new church in Roman Road.

34. Ingatestone Hall. The Gatehouse seen from the rear. A familiar sight to thousands of visitors leaving the Hall. For 25 years part had been leased to the Essex Record Office and opened to the public for annual exhibitions.

35. Lime Walk, in the grounds of Ingatestone Hall. Mrs. Braddon, the immensely popular Victorian novelist, who stayed for a time at the Hall, wrote a best-seller — 'Lady Audley's Secret' — based on the house. Part of the plot involves a murder in the Walk and the disposal of the body in the well (this link explains the popularity of the postcard). A hundred years earlier the Walk had been the scene of a real-life adventure, when Bishop Petre was attacked by robbers and his life saved by a large black dog.

36. Boys' School in Fryerning Lane (the site is now Steen Close — named after a local doctor). The centre shows the Drill Hall, erected before the Second World War, and later converted into an engineering factory. Further left can be seen council houses. The school, originally known as Fryerning School, was built in 1873. In 1904, when George West was headmaster, there were hundred boys on the register. It was demolished in 1964 when the new Church of England School was built in the Furlongs.

37. Ingatestone Old Rectory. Rectors had lived here for many centuries. When the new Rectory was built in Fryerning Lane, it was sold to Mr. C. Twining Sidgwick (chairman of the tea company). He lived there for 57 years. The property, immediately behind the church, now covered by the Fairfield estate (1968) included three acres of garden.

38. Docklands. One of the many private houses with large grounds built in the nineteenth century. It had no special history, and was demolished to make way for Docklands Avenue and adjoining roads.

INGATESTONE STATION.

39. Station Yard c. 1910. In the centre is the postman with his barrow. Moy's coal office is also seen, and a horse-drawn dray. No parked cars! The gentry were driven to the station in carriages, others walked.

40. Troops. The High Street has been the scene of troop movements from the earliest
times. This card, taken by Avenue Terrace, is of the Royal Artillery in the First World
War, probably on the way to embarkation. (Courts martial were once held in an upper
room of The Crown, which still bears regimental markings.)

41. Mr. Archibald Christy, an architect who built and lived at Wellmead in Fryerning Lane, formed the first scouting troop in 1908. He is seen six years later at camp. The Hall, in Pemberton Avenue, named after the Christy family, was built in 1974 after years of voluntary effort.

42. Part of the Armistice parade through the High Street in 1919. On the extreme left stands Mr. Freddy Sorrell, postman of Stock outside the Forge (demolished c. 1967 and now the jewellers). On the right, the protruding window of Rose's sweet shop; on the extreme right what was originally The Ship Inn, later a cycle shop. It was subsequently demolished and the site is now the entrance to the car park.

43. George Sherrin. Eminent Victorian architect; he was born in London but spent much of his life at Ingatestone. He designed, and lived, in the Gate House, in Station Lane (see No. 30). He had an extremely busy practice, and at one time is said to have had sixty commissions in hand. He designed many of the larger houses in Ingatestone and Fryerning, and was also responsible for several London Underground stations, departmental stores, and Southend's Kursaal. His son, Frank, succeeded to his practice, and he too designed a number of local buildings.

44. Cricket team c. 1930 outside the pavilion. From left to right, back row: Smith, S. Pinnock, G. Pinkey, G. Downes, Stanford and J. Sitch. Front row: E.A. Myward, B. Ungles, B. Clark (captain), W. Raven and C.H. Cox.

45. Buttsbury Church. An example of England's many thousand deserted churches. The village once surrounding it has completely disappeared. Damaged by a bomb in the Second World War and restored — the mainly fourteenth century interior has a wonderful sense of tranquility. The transept (on left) housed a boiler for heating and now features a beautiful traceried window.

46. Fryerning Green. A scene virtually unchanged in the eighty years since this photograph was taken (except for the donkey!). The massive oak tree in the grounds of Fryerning Hall is at least eight hundred years old.

FRYERING INGATESTONE. 800.

47. Grange Road (now called Back Lane) looking towards Writtle. The white posts fenced in the moat of Huskards. The elm trees have gone. Adkins, in the centre backgrond, is one of the oldest and most interesting houses in Fryerning, and dates from 1325. The coach house of Huskards is on the left.

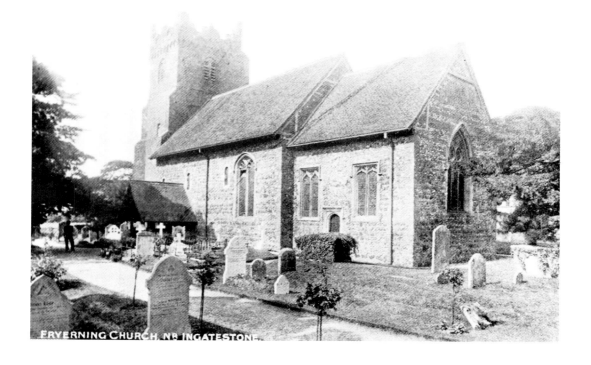

FRYERNING CHURCH, NR INGATESTONE.

48. Fryerning Church. The nave has not been enlarged since it was built nine hundred years ago, and the church still holds a little over a hundred people. The walls are three feet thick. The fine brick tower was added in the early sixteenth century, about the same time and in the same style as Ingatestone's.

49. Fryerning Church interior. The church was drastically restored in 1869. The photograph was taken before the introduction of electric lighting, before the oak panelling covering the eastern wall of the sanctuary was fitted in 1910, and before the dominating oak rood separating nave and chancel was added as a memorial to the dead of 1914-1918. It shows, behind the altar, the stone reredos, now covered by hangings.

"Trueloves" Igatestone. -92962

50. Trueloves (for a time known as Ingatestone Court). There has been a house on this site since at least the seventeenth century. Around 1900 it was practically pulled down and rebuilt in the Elizabethan style. During the 1920's (Sir) Hubert Ashton lived here, and later, for many years it was one of the five residential schools of the Shaftesbury Society.

51. Huskards. There was originally a mediaeval hall house which was demolished in the eighteenth century and rebuilt. It has been very much altered by its many owners. The last private family to live there were the Hilders. During the First World War it was used as a convalescent home for the wounded. It later became an old people's home, and in 1978 was converted into flats.

Fred Spalding
Photo Chelmsford

52. The Hyde, in New Road in 1904. A splendid mansion set in a well-timbered park of two hundred acres. It contained an outstanding collection of antiquities, most of which were donated to Cambridge University. The Disney family owned the house. In 1950 it became a school, but fifteen years later was destroyed by fire, thought to have been started by a disgruntled servant. Only part of the entrance, and a short length of wall remain.

53. Fryerning Rectory. A view of the rear from the croquet lawn. An impressive red-brick Georgian house with six bedrooms, and two acres of grounds. It had not always been the Rectory; A.P. (Bunny) Lucas, the famous England and Essex cricketer, lived here for a time. Sold by auction in 1979 for £105,000, it was almost completely rebuilt.

WOOLPACK. FRYERNING

54. The Woolpack, adjoining Fryerning Green. One of Fryerning's three inns, it was, a few years ago, renamed The Huntsman. An annual fair was held on the Green. The name 'Woolpack' had been attached to other inns. The present building is only about hundred years old. It had the distinction, before boundary changes, of being in both Ingatestone and Fryerning.

55. Mill Green Road c. 1908, looking towards the Mill in the distance. The only buildings that can be seen are Maygotts and what is now the Gospel Hall. The watertower had not then been built. Note the state of the unmade roads.

56. The post-mill from which Mill Green takes its name. It now stands in the grounds of a private house (Millhurst). Last used around 1900, it had, by 1959 become a wreck, but twenty years later was completely restored.

57. Mill Green. Post office and Cricketers. The post office, like that of Margaretting, has gone, though the house remains.

THE VIPER, MILL GREEN

58. The Viper at Mill Green. Possibly the only inn in England named after this snake, and so-called from the vipers which are to be found in this heavily wooded area.

MARGARETTING VILLAGE, Nᴮ INGATESTONE.

59. Margaretting. Main road, looking towards Chelmsford c. 1910.

60. Margaretting. Scene opposite The Bull Inn in 1900. Three generations of the Bartrop family were proprietors of a general store. All buildings and trees have gone, and in their place a new house was built around 1910 (see No. 65).

ST. MARGARET. MARGARETTING. 1708.

61. Margaretting Church. It is the most interesting one in the area covered by this book; with three distinctive features — a wealth of mediaeval carpentry, a rare Jesse east window, and a unique, pre-Reformation set of four bells. The untidy hedge and summer-house, which were part of the vicarage garden, have gone.

THE VICARAGE, MARGARETTING. 11590

62. Margaretting vicarage. Standing immediately to the side of the church, it was for centuries occupied by the vicars of Margaretting (in 1958 the parish was united with Fryerning and the new vicar/rector lived at Fryerning Rectory). The charming grey-bricked house, in private hands, was added in 1822 to the original vicarage, still adjoined.

63. Margaretting post office in 1900. It remained a post office till c. 1912, when the office was transferred to various places, finally closing c. 1970.

MARGARETTING . 729 .

64. Margaretting. Red Lion. Five hundred years old and boasting 150 varieties of whisky, this inn has changed little over the centuries. It once belonged to the Disney family.

65. Margaretting. The general store was rebuilt around 1910 (see No. 60) and is now in private ownership.

66. Margaretting. Peacocks. A 'charming stuccoed Regency house' in a beautiful setting. It is so charming that one expects it to be peopled with Jane Austen characters. Now the home of Lord and Lady Chelmer.

67. Mountnessing, from Church Road. The pond facing the Roman Road has been filled in and there is now a small garden. The well supplied five old cottages.

"PLOUGH", MOUNTNESSING

68. Mountnessing, The Plough. Now replaced by a larger and less attractive building. The small cottage next to the inn has gone and the houses further left have been very much altered.

69. Mountnessing Church, standing two hundred feet above sea-level. Although approximately in the centre of the parish, it is two miles from the main Colchester Road, where the village now clusters. The church porch has been added since the photograph was taken.

70. Mountnessing 'Tin' Church. Because of the distance of his church from the centre of the village, the Reverend Richard Macnamara, vicar, in 1873 erected a small iron church (which held about two hundred people) close to the main road. The pews were taken out about 1970, but it is still in use sometimes as a church and sometimes for secular purposes. The photograph shows a well laid-out garden and rose trees.

71. Mountnessing. Windmill. Awaiting repairs 1938. A noted landmark on the Roman Road. It is a typical post-mill of the early nineteenth century. Between 1817 and 1937 it was worked by four successive generations of the Agnis family. They all lived in the Mill House shown on the left. A new house re-named Mill Cottage was built a few yards further away in Thoby Lane. Thanks to the Friends of the Windmill, the mill is now completely restored and in working order.

Thoby Priory. Mountnessing.

72. Mountnessing. Thoby Priory. Founded in the twelfth century, it was named after the first prior, Tobias or Toby. Wolsey appropriated it in order to endow colleges. It was then demolished and rebuilt as a private house, incorporating some of the original fabric. There was a serious fire in 1893 and it was again rebuilt. In 1920 it was bought by the Earl of Arran, famous as a newspaper columnist. Some thirty, fourty years later it was inexcusably demolished. Two arches are all that remain of the original priory. The whole site is now covered by a vast scrap-metal yard!

MOUNTNESSING. 536.

73. Mountnessing, Roman Road. The Albert Cottages on the left have gone, as well as the small protruding roof of the blacksmith's. The Prince of Wales is on the right.

The Schools. Mountnessing.

74. Mountnessing School, boys and girls around 1920. The exterior is virtually unchanged today, except that the hands of the clock, and the roof turrets, have gone.

75. Mountnessing, war memorial. A great day in the life of the village — the service of dedication of the memorial to the fallen of the Great War, 1920. The vicar, the Reverend Henry Cobbing, conducts the service. To his left in the choir are Lionel Goodday and Chris Read. The seated figure on the right is Walter Agnis, mill-owner, who lost two sons in the war. They are the first two names on the memorial.

76. Mountnessing, farm workers at the completion of the harvest. Taken at Arnolds Farm
at the turn of the century. The men worked three farms Beagrams, Jordans and Arnolds.
Note the gaiters and variety of headgear worn.